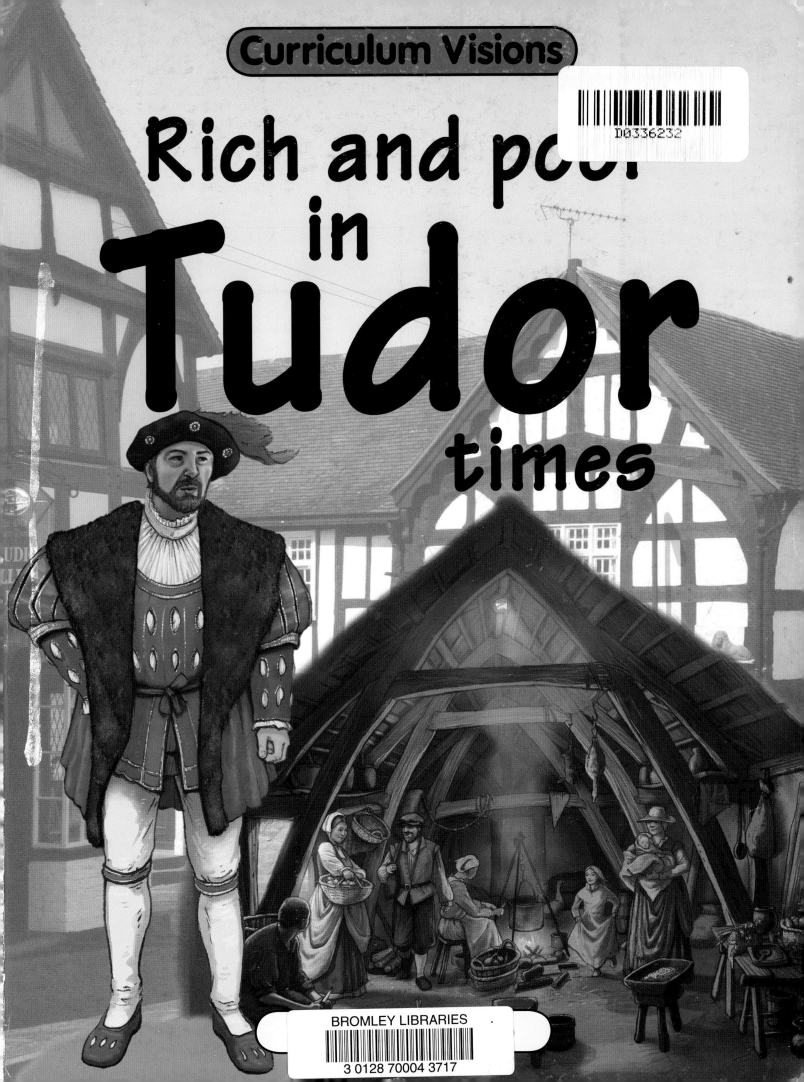

Rich and poor in Tudor times

▼ A Tudor coaching inn, Ludlow.

Curriculum Visions

Curriculum Visions is a registered trademark of Atlantic Europe Publishing Company Ltd.

There's more on-line

There's more about other great Curriculum Visions packs and a wealth of supporting information available at our dedicated web site. Visit:

www.CurriculumVisions.com

Atlantic Europe Publishing

First published in 2005 by
Atlantic Europe Publishing Company Ltd.
Copyright © 2005
Atlantic Europe Publishing Company Ltd.
First reprint 2005. Second reprint 2006.

Author
Brian Knapp, BSc, PhD

Editor
Robert Anderson, BA, PGCE

Art Director
Duncan McCrae, BSc

Designed and produced by
EARTHSCAPE EDITIONS

Senior Designer
Adele Humphries, BA, PGCE

Printed in China by
WKT Company Ltd

Rich and poor in Tudor times – *Curriculum Visions*
A CIP record for this book is available from the British Library

Paperback ISBN-10: 1-86214-428-1
Paperback ISBN-10: 978-1-86214-428-6

Hardback ISBN-13: 1-86214-430-3
Hardback ISBN-13: 978-1-86214-430-9

Illustrations (c=centre t=top b=bottom l=left r=right)
Mark Stacey cover illustrations, pages 6–7, 8–9, 10–11, 12, 13, 15, 16, 18, 19, 21, 26, 28, 30–31, 32, 33b, 34, 35, 36, 38–39, 40, 44; *David Woodroffe* page 25.

Picture credits
All photographs are from the Earthscape Editions photolibrary except the following: (c=centre t=top b=bottom l=left r=right) *The Granger Collection, New York* pages 4, 22, 42, 43t, 43b, 45bl; *Hereford Museum* pages 33tr, 33cl; © *National Maritime Museum, London* page 24.

⚠ Look after our heritage!

It is easy to talk about looking after the environment, but we each have to help. Help is often small things, like being careful when you walk around old buildings, and not leaving scratch marks on anything that you visit. It doesn't take a lot of effort – just attitude.

Contents

▼ What living in a Tudor town might have been like.

▼ **INTRODUCTION**
4   Tudor times

▼ **TUDOR TIMES TO HENRY VIII**
6   A big gap between rich and poor
8   A land of small villages
10 Our village in 1500
12 Homes in the village
14 Village life
16 Farmland changes
18 Our town in 1500
20 The great Tudor houses
22 The Church loses its wealth

THE TIMES OF QUEEN ELIZABETH I AND AFTER
24 Francis Drake and the Armada
26 Our village in 1600
28 Our town in 1600
30 Inside a Tudor town house
32 Furniture and fittings
34 What the Tudors ate and drank
36 Almshouse and workhouse
38 Plague
40 Learning
42 Exploration
44 Settlers

▼ **REFERENCE**
46 Words, names and places
48 Index

Words in **CAPITALS** are further explained under 'Words, places and names' on pages 46–47.

▲ A Tudor tankard made from pewter.

Tudor times

This book is about rich and poor Tudors – people who lived during times when many famous English kings and queens, including Henry VIII and Elizabeth I, were on the throne.

The first of the **TUDOR** kings and queens (monarchs) was **HENRY VII**, also known as Henry Tudor. He became king in 1485, when he and his troops won the Battle of Bosworth. His reign began one of the most famous periods of English history – the time of the Tudors.

On this page you will learn briefly about what happened during Tudor times. The rest of the book tells you how life changed for better and worse during Tudor times.

❶ In 1485, Henry Tudor became king of England and Wales (Henry VII, Henry the Seventh). He was a hard-working and serious man.

❷ When Henry VII died, his son **HENRY VIII** (Henry the Eighth) became king. His reign lasted from 1509 to 1547. Henry was a very scheming and clever man.

▲ ① Elizabeth I was the most famous Tudor queen.

❸ When Henry VIII died, his son **EDWARD VI** (Edward the Sixth) became king for just six years.

❹ In 1553, Edward's eldest sister, Mary, became queen (**MARY I**, Mary the First). She was a talented ruler, but had an even shorter reign – from 1553 to 1558.

❺ When Mary died, her sister, **ELIZABETH I** (Elizabeth the First), became queen (picture ①). She had a very long reign, from 1558 to 1603. Elizabeth was a brave and clever woman. Elizabeth was the last of the Tudors.

6 During Tudor times the number of people in England and Wales grew quickly. They needed more food, so people who owned land became wealthier selling food. This was the time when many fine Tudor houses were built (picture ②).

7 Some people were forced off their land. They left the countryside and went to towns to seek work. But there were more workers than jobs, so many of these people were poor, homeless and starving.

▼ ② **During Tudor times, wool towns, in particular, became prosperous and new buildings were constructed. These are among the oldest buildings still standing today. Earlier Tudor houses had exposed oak beams. Later houses were made of stone.**

Tudor timeline of important events

1485	Henry Tudor is the first Tudor king. England has three million people.
1492	CHRISTOPHER COLUMBUS arrives in America (the 'New World') from Spain.
1509	Henry VIII becomes king.
1534	Parliament agrees to break with the ROMAN CATHOLIC CHURCH and start a new PROTESTANT Church of England.
1537 –1539	Henry VIII closes the MONASTERIES.
1547	Edward VI becomes king.
1553	Mary I becomes queen. Three hundred Protestants are burned at the stake.
1554	PEASANTS revolt against Mary's Roman Catholic ideas.
1558	Elizabeth I becomes queen. England is Protestant again.
1564	The playright WILLIAM SHAKESPEARE is born.
1577	SIR FRANCIS DRAKE begins his voyage around the world. It takes two years.
1585	The East India Company is founded to begin trading for silk and spices with Asia.
1586	SIR WALTER RALEIGH brings tobacco from North America to England.
1587	MARY, QUEEN OF SCOTS is executed.
1588	Sir Francis Drake defeats the Spanish ARMADA and prevents an invasion by Spain.
1603	Elizabeth I dies. England has four million people.

A big gap between rich and poor

Nothing better showed who was rich and who was poor than the clothes people wore.

In Tudor times, there were very few wealthy people and a large number of poor people. Rich and poor dressed very differently.

How rich ladies dressed

The rich were very keen to be seen in the latest clothes and the newest styles (picture ①).

In early Tudor times, ladies wore long gowns with wide sleeves. In middle Tudor times, the fashion was to wear gowns drawn in at the waist using strips of metal or whalebone. The skirt was held out by hoops.

In late Tudor times, ladies had to suffer being drawn in even more at the waist, making them look almost wasp-like in shape. They wore a ruff around the neck (see picture ① on page 4).

◄ ① During Tudor times the rich dressed according to fashion. This is the fashion as it was in the time of Henry VIII.

How wealthy men dressed

At the start of Tudor times, rich young men wore white silk shirts, frilled at the neck and wrists. Over this they wore a tunic and close-fitting striped trousers (called **HOSE**). Older men wore gowns to cover up their fat stomachs. Everyone wore their hair shoulder length.

By middle Tudor times, men had padded arm puffs and everyone had a short velvet gown. Hair was now shorter, and small beards were fashionable.

By late Tudor times, men's trousers ballooned out just below the waist. A ruff was now worn around the neck.

How poorer people dressed

For the poor, fashion didn't change at all (picture ②). Many of their clothes were made at home.

Most men wore a hose of wool and a tunic that came down to just above the knees. Some had a **DOUBLET**; most wore a soft hat. Women wore a dress of wool that went down to the ground. They often wore an apron over this and a cloth bonnet on their heads.

◀ ② The style of dress for the poor remained much the same throughout Tudor times.

A land of small villages

When Tudor times started, England was in a poor state. Nobody would have guessed that, within a century, England would be among the world's wealthiest nations.

What was England like when Henry VII, the first of the Tudors, became king in 1485?

When Tudor times began, England had only three million people (there are nearly 49 million today). There were far more sheep than people – in fact, about three sheep to every person.

There were no large towns or cities. Even London was small.

If you could have flown over the coast you would have seen only small fishing villages with tiny sailing ships at anchor. There would be no big fleet of ships, for England was too poor.

If you could have flown across the land you would have seen little villages next to castles and abbeys (pictures ① and ②). Each village had meadows beside the river, and huge 'thousand acre' fields where people grew their crops in long, thin strips (strip fields).

But most of all you would have seen forest (pictures ① and ③). Forest covered far more land than fields did. In these forests you would occasionally also have seen clearings where men were making iron. They were using the trees as fuel.

Why England was so backward

For four centuries, since the time of **WILLIAM THE CONQUEROR**, barons and other powerful people had each run their own part of the country, fighting and squabbling among themselves. The king had also fought long costly wars with France. England had also lost many people through disease and starvation.

The result was that England was poorer and more backward than its neighbours in Europe.

▲ ③ In 1500 much of England was still covered by forest. A few people went hunting in the forests, but for most it was a gloomy and fearful place.

▲ ① Most people lived in villages close to rivers or next to the sea.

▶ ② At the start of Tudor times, the wealthy still mainly lived behind thick castle walls because they were afraid of being attacked.

Our village in 1500

In 1500, most people lived in countryside villages. Over the next few pages we'll take a look at what one such village might have been like.

Our village is very old. It might have been founded hundreds of years earlier by **ANGLO-SAXONS** or **VIKINGS**. Since then the village has grown a bit, and a new church was built a couple of hundred years ago. By and large, however, it hasn't changed very much since **MEDIEVAL TIMES** (picture ①).

Because the roads are very poor, most people prefer to travel by boat to nearby towns and villages.

▶ ① Our village is next to a river. The route across the river is still guarded by a castle. The biggest building in the village is the church. All other buildings are small. Few are made of good-quality materials.

The chimneys were added to this hall house in later Tudor times. The barn (to the right) has also been made part of the house.

Many buildings combine a house with a barn. There are no chimneys — only a hole in the roof lets the smoke out.

The houses are mostly made up of a single room with earth floors and thatch roof. The wooden frame is filled in with twigs and plastered with mud, cow dung, hair and straw (wattle and daub).

Large fields surround the village. They are divided into strips, and each farmer has a number of strips in different fields. One field is always left unploughed, or fallow, to give the soil a chance to recover after producing a crop. Beyond the fields is forest.

The mill is important because it is where people grind their grain.

The church is the largest building. It might still have an Anglo-Saxon tower. Most likely, however, it would have been rebuilt during **NORMAN TIMES** and all traces of the Anglo-Saxon church would have been destroyed.

The 'hall house' – the biggest house in the village – is home to a rich **YEOMAN**.

The paths in the village are muddy and covered in animal and human waste.

From time to time, markets are held in an open space in the village.

Many homes have a small patch of land for growing vegetables and keeping pigs and chickens.

Near by is a castle, where the rich rulers live.

Weblink: www.CurriculumVisions.com

Homes in the village

Most people lived in poorly built hovels. Only a few had fine houses.

In our village most of the houses and land are owned by the **LORD OF THE MANOR** and an **ABBOT**. These powerful people take rents from the **PEASANTS** who live in their houses, and they also get a tenth part (called a **TITHE**) of everything the peasants grow.

The lord lives in a large hall house in the village. But the abbot lives a long way away in an abbey. The Church owns lots of land.

Our village also has a few better-off people. They are called **YEOMEN**. They own their own houses (picture ①). You can spot where they live in picture ① on pages 10 and 11 – their houses are much larger and better kept than the others. The houses the yeomen rent out to peasants are very different – most of them are falling into ruin.

▼ ① Yeomen were beginning to become wealthy by the start of Tudor times. This yeoman's hall house is still standing, though the extra floor and chimney were added later.

▼▶ ② **Many Tudor buildings were based on an arch frame made of leaning beams. This is called a cruck frame.**

Village homes

No matter what their size, most houses in our village consist of a single room.

Each home is made using a frame of timber posts (picture ②). They are cut from the nearby forest. The walls of the poorer homes are made with straw, dung, mud and twigs. It is called **WATTLE AND DAUB**. The richer villagers have walls made with strips of wood called **LATHS** covered with **PLASTER**.

Inside, the floor is earth. There is no built fireplace and no chimney. The fire is simply made on the floor in the centre of the room. Its smoke makes the whole house black with soot. There is no ceiling. You look straight up to the roof.

In a few houses there is a loft over part of the room to store food out of the reach of rats.

Behind each house is a kitchen garden for growing vegetables and keeping animals. There is also a dung heap, which stinks!

Using the room

The room is used for sleeping and eating as well as for jobs like weaving.

There is no question of keeping it clean or keeping the rats out. So our village houses are filthy, inside and out. But as no one knows about hygiene and disease, this doesn't worry our villagers.

Weblink: www.CurriculumVisions.com

Village life

Our village has to look after its own affairs, including law and order.

The church is the biggest building in the village (picture ①). But it is not the clean, tidy building that we are used to today. Instead, the floor is strewn with straw because when there are no services, animals are kept in the church. The straw is also useful because during the long sermons people often go to the toilet just where they are sitting!

The hall

Our village has a hall. This is not a grand building, but simply a room where the officials of the lord meet with the villagers when their rents are due.

Arguments between people or wrongdoings are also settled by a court held in the hall. It is run by the lord's **STEWARD**. The **BAILIFF** is there to carry out the decision of the steward.

The market

Our villagers grow most of the food they want and make most of the goods they need (picture ②).

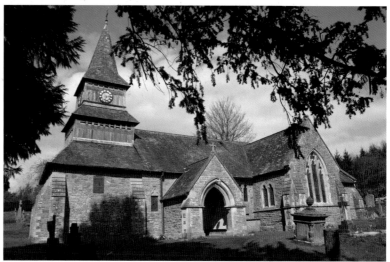

▲ ① This church was built in the 13th century (1200s).

But there is a space for a weekly market where bakers, fishmongers and butchers can bring their goods to be sold (picture ③).

Trades

Most people weave cloth or do some other kind of work after they come back from the fields. A few people have a full-time trade.

▼ ② The mill, powered by the river, was a very important building. Everyone's corn was ground here.

▲ ③ Our village has an open space with a covered area for a market. Punishments for wrongdoing are carried out here.

The water in the stream is polluted and cannot be used for drinking. As a result, people all drink weak beer, because brewing destroys the germs in the water. Not surprisingly, the most common trade is beermaking.

The village also has a tanner and a candlemaker. They boil up the hides and fat of dead animals to make leather and candles. This is a smelly job, and so they have to live on the downwind edge of the village.

The streets

The streets are no more than paths. Their surfaces are made from beaten earth. They are so rarely mended that they are pitted with holes. In winter, the road is a sea of mud in which carts regularly get stuck.

There is nowhere to put rubbish and nowhere special to go to the toilet. As a result everything finds its way into the gutter that runs down the middle of the street – and then into the stream. The stench in summer is terrible.

Some of the poorest people sort through the rubbish and pile it up when they have finished, so they know which piles have been sorted. These piles are called mire heaps.

Unfortunately, nobody realises that the dung and much of the other mess that litters the roads would make a valuable and free fertiliser. So no one thinks of taking it away to the fields.

Weblink: www.CurriculumVisions.com

Farmland changes

During early Tudor times, the way people farmed the land began to change.

For centuries, the land around our village has been farmed in huge fields (picture ①).

Each farmer has a few narrow strips scattered across three great fields. After the harvest, animals graze in the fields.

Most of the land is owned by the lord and the Church, but a little of it is owned by the yeomen. The peasants have to rent land.

From strips to fields

Growing crops in strips the ancient way does not make enough money in Tudor England. Those who own land know they can make more money by grazing sheep and selling their wool than by renting it to peasants. So they have decided to get rid of the ploughed strips and turn the land over to grazing.

▼ ① **Farming provides many people with a living, but they hardly make any profit.**

Recently, after harvest one year, the owners got together and shared out the land into small rectangular fields (picture ②). This is called **ENCLOSURE**.

The yeomen are building new homes on their land. These are the very first farmhouses to be built away from the villages.

Big changes

The edges of the new fields need to be marked. Deep ditches are dug across the land and the soil from the ditches thrown up to make ridges. On the ridges, hawthorn and other trees are planted to make hedges.

Poor peasants

What say do the peasants have in these decisions?

They have no say. After the harvest they were simply told that they can't have the land for ploughing or growing their food any longer. All they can do is to become workers for the farmers who now own the fields. Or they can leave and go to look for work in the town. So a few more people move to the town, which therefore gets a bit larger. And a few more village hovels become unused and rot away.

▼ ② Enclosing the land makes a few people wealthier and many poorer.

Our town in 1500

Towns were rare in 1500. But our town is set to grow.

Near our village is a bigger place. We shall call it our town (picture ①). The town has grown up where two rivers meet. It was first settled nearly a thousand years before, just like our village.

The town by the abbey

The main building in the town is an **ABBEY**. The abbot and the monks that live there need food, clothes, shoes, horses and many other things. This gives work to the townspeople.

Pilgrims frequently visit the abbey. Providing them with board and lodging gives more work to the townspeople.

Living and working

Even though this is a town, each house has a long strip of land behind it. This is where people grow vegetables and keep animals such as pigs and chickens.

▼ ① Our town.

Abbey

Merchant's house

Inn

Strip fields

Wharf

Marketplace

Basketmaker's

Brewer's

Mill

Tannery

Potter's   Brickmaker's

▲ ② Buildings had to serve as workshops and storerooms as well as homes. Look at the doors in the upper floor. This is where goods were loaded and unloaded on to carts.

The main street leads from the abbey to a ford across the river (in later years a bridge will be built).

If you are a wealthy merchant, a squire, a lawyer or a very skilled craftsman, you may be able to afford to live at the end of the town nearest the abbey (pictures ②, ③ and ④).

Houses become cheaper towards the outskirts. So next come the highly skilled weavers, bakers, tailors, **CUTLERS** and gunsmiths. They can all afford to own their houses.

Beyond this the houses are rented. They are smaller and more cramped, hardly more than thatched sheds. Here more sewage and filth build up.

This is also where foul-smelling trades take place or those that can cause fire. This is where you can find potters, blacksmiths, butchers, brewers, coopers, skinners, tanners, candlemakers and brickmakers.

On the very edge of town live the poorest people of all – the 'night soil carriers' (sewage collectors).

At some distance outside the town you would see, but not go near, the **LEPERS**.

▲ ③ In prosperous towns, covered markets were built using massive oak posts. Nearby was the inn.

▲ ④ The street plans of Tudor towns still survive today in some modern town centres.

The great Tudor houses

By Tudor times, the rich no longer needed castles to protect themselves, so they built grand new houses. Some were really palaces.

▲ ① **Early Tudor houses were built around a courtyard. Hampton Court is the biggest of these. Later houses were built in H or E shapes.**

For centuries, the rich lived in castles because they were afraid for their safety. But in Tudor times, people wanted something more comfortable than a draughty stone castle. They also wanted to use the latest materials – brick and glass (pictures ① and ②).

Many of these new houses were built in the countryside. Some of them were the size of palaces.

The great country house

For thousands of years, people had lived in a single all-purpose room with a fire in the middle.

▲ ② **St James's Palace in London was built for Henry VIII. It is built of brick – a symbol of wealth at a time when bricks were expensive.**

Everything changed when chimneys were invented in Tudor times. Many fires could now be lit, and the single room divided into many separate rooms, each of which could be used for a different purpose.

The rich could now live in private on one side of the hall, while the servants were housed on the other side.

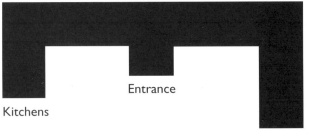

▲▼ ③ The long gallery was not a living room. It was a place where people could display works of art, tapestries and furniture. It was also a place where they could show off their fine clothes to each other, or simply talk in private.

Hall   Long gallery (upper floor)

Entrance

Kitchens

Living area

To show off their fine belongings, a room was added running along the whole side of the house. It was called a long gallery (picture ③).

The grand town house

There was no room in a town for spacious buildings like those being built in the country. Instead, buildings were designed with many floors.

Servants and masters could still live separately. The master and his family lived on the ground and first floors, leaving the basement and the attic for the servants.

The Church loses its wealth

The Church owned a huge amount of land and got wealthy on the rents it collected. Everything changed, though, in the time of Henry VIII.

In 1500, the Church was more powerful and wealthier than the king.

The Church in England was part of the **ROMAN CATHOLIC CHURCH**. It got its instructions from the pope in Rome, Italy. The pope had a huge influence over what happened in England.

Henry VIII

Henry VIII, like most kings of England, was short of money (picture ①). He could not afford to pay his army properly or do many of the other things he wanted.

For many years Henry remained loyal to the Roman Catholic Church. But he needed a boy heir. His first wife, **CATHERINE OF ARAGON**, had not given him this. So after ten years he wanted to divorce her and marry **ANNE BOLEYN**, who he hoped would bear him a son.

When the pope refused to let Henry divorce Catherine, Henry decided to break away from the Church in Rome and become a **PROTESTANT**. He made himself head of the Church in England, and seized all of the Church lands and wealth.

▲ ① Henry VIII wanted to get rid of the Roman Catholic Church because he could take over their wealth and influence.

Abbeys are destroyed

Henry ordered the destruction of important Catholic buildings such as abbeys and monasteries (picture ②). The event is known as the **DISSOLUTION OF THE MONASTERIES**.

The abbey in our town was among the buildings destroyed. The lead from the roof was ripped off and the stone from the walls used to make other buildings.

Many wealthy merchants were eager to buy land so they could build their own country houses. This is one reason why England has so many grand country houses today.

New manors formed

Henry had no use for the Church lands. But he knew he could divide up the land and sell it for a profit.

▼▶ ② Abbeys were made uninhabitable by smashing roofs and windows. Local people then took the stone to use in their own buildings. This is why so many abbeys lie in ruins. This is Valle Crucis in Wales.

Francis Drake and the Armada

England was often threatened by her neighbours. The biggest threat of all came from Spain, which was rich and powerful.

England was still quite a poor and weak country compared to other countries like Spain.

In order to protect his kingdom, however, Henry VIII built up a large navy – the Royal Navy.

Edward, Mary and Elizabeth

When Henry VIII died, England was a **PROTESTANT** country. Henry's son, who then became King Edward VI, was also a Protestant.

When Edward died, the throne was taken by his sister Mary. Mary turned England back into a Catholic country. But within a few years, Mary, too, was dead and her Protestant sister, Elizabeth, was on the throne.

Spain plans to invade

Elizabeth had no love for Spain – which was a Catholic country – and England still needed money. So Elizabeth allowed **SIR FRANCIS DRAKE** (see pages 42–43) and his fleet to attack Spanish ships in the **WEST INDIES** and plunder their wealth.

The king of Spain, Philip II, decided to remove Elizabeth from the throne of England and return the country to the Catholic faith. To do this, he brought together a fleet of 130 ships called the **ARMADA**. By 1588, the ships were ready to go to collect an army from Calais and carry it across the English Channel.

▼ ① **Elizabeth knew that she could not defeat the massive Spanish army on land. Twenty-two GALLEONS, as well as many smaller ships, sailed in the Armada. Food for the expedition included 5 million kg of ships biscuits and 300,000 kg of salt pork. The only way to stop it was to destroy the Armada at sea. Fortunately, among her fleet commanders was Sir Francis Drake – a very skilful leader.**

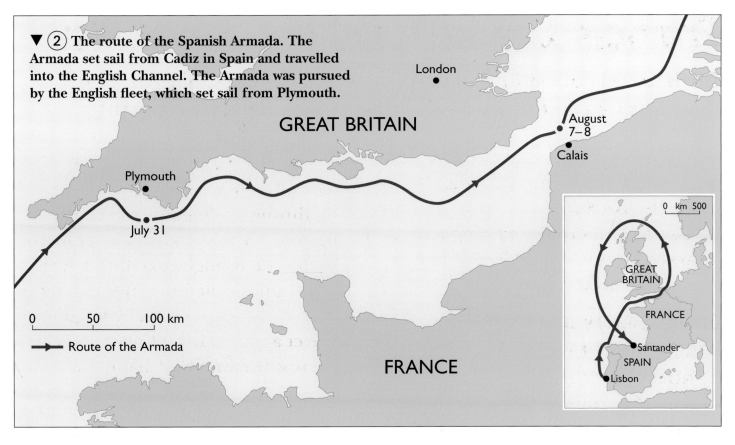

▼ ② The route of the Spanish Armada. The Armada set sail from Cadiz in Spain and travelled into the English Channel. The Armada was pursued by the English fleet, which set sail from Plymouth.

London

GREAT BRITAIN

August 7–8

Calais

Plymouth

July 31

0   50   100 km

→ Route of the Armada

FRANCE

0   km   500

GREAT BRITAIN

FRANCE

Santander

SPAIN

Lisbon

Big guns

As the Armada sailed into the English Channel, the English fleet sailed out from Plymouth in Devon (pictures ① and ②). Who would win the battle depended on the speed of the ships, the number and size of guns, the skill of the admiral in charge and, finally, the weather.

The English fleet was smaller than the Armada. It had about 100 ships. However, the English ships were faster and had guns that could be reloaded more quickly than those of the Spanish. The Spanish only had 40 battle ships among their fleet. All of the rest were for carrying soldiers. The English fleet was about 100 ships, but all of these were suited to battle.

Fireships

When the Armada anchored off Calais to wait for the soldiers from land, the English launched eight fireships at the Spanish fleet. This forced them to cut their anchors and move out to sea to avoid catching fire. The English attacked, sinking one Spanish ship and driving two ashore.

Bad weather

The westerly winds also quickly drove the rest of the Armada out into the North Sea. To escape, the Armada now had to sail round the British Isles. The weather was terrible, and only 60 ships returned to Spain (picture ② inset). Some 15,000 men were drowned when their ships sank. The Spanish invasion had been defeated.

Our village in 1600

During Tudor times England prospered. Villages and towns grew quickly, and many new buildings were constructed.

During the time of Queen Elizabeth I – the second half of the sixteenth century – our village changes quickly. This is because some people in England are getting much richer.

The Great Rebuilding

As these wealthy people set about rebuilding their villages, so the face of our villages changes for ever. This is the time called the **GREAT REBUILDING** (picture ①).

Some people rebuild the inside of their houses or add an extra room to the back of their homes.

Others knock their houses down completely and start all over again. The new house is both bigger and better quality.

But most important, people begin to change what they use buildings for. Instead of using one room for everything, they keep their animals in a separate barn. For the first time, people live alone in their homes.

▼ ① Compare our village now with the village at the start of Tudor times (pages 10 to 11). What do you notice?

Homes that stand the test of time

The time of the Great Rebuilding produced sturdy small houses. Many of the pretty thatched or tiled cottages we see today were built as yeoman's houses at this time (pictures ②, ③ and ④).

What happened to the poor?

There was, however, no money for the houses of the poor. In our village their houses remain hovels. Within a century, they will have fallen down, which is why we see no trace of them today.

▲ ② Some people added an extra floor to their house by dividing the existing house. This is why some houses have very low ceilings.

◄ ③ This is a new yeoman's house built completely of stone. Its windows are bigger than those of earlier houses.

▼ ④ This is a yeoman's house rebuilt with a traditional wooden frame filled with brick. It has a stone base.

Weblink: www.CurriculumVisions.com

Our town in 1600

As people left the villages, towns grew in size. But there was not always a better living to be found.

In our town new houses are being built by merchants, with workshops below and a place to live above (picture ①). Inns and other places for travellers are being built in the centre of the town because more people are now travelling about the country (pictures ② and ③).

More goods are being made, so there is a need for more people to make them – provided they are willing to work for low wages.

From village to town

A town hall has been built over the covered market. A growing town needs more and more food, so the market has changed from once a week to every day. But our town still has no shops – these will not come for 200 years.

▼ ① The main street in our town is a mixture of workshops and inns lining a muddy road. The town is crowded with people bringing goods to market.

Crowding

To fit in more houses, people are building on the land behind their houses, which they once used for growing vegetables and keeping pigs.

To get to these new houses, narrow alleys are made from the roads. In these side alleys, houses are being built so close that people on opposite sides of the alley can lean out their windows and touch each other. It is a recipe for disaster if fire should ever break out. Crowded houses also make it more likely that disease will spread (see pages 38–39).

Despite these changes, in some ways the town is still part of the country. Some people still keep their cattle in byres behind their houses. They take them to the meadows by the river during the day and bring them back through the town alleys at night.

Showing off your wealth

The rich show off their wealth by building more chimneys, using more glass and having larger windows than their neighbours. If you are very very wealthy, you can now also get running water and a toilet.

▲ ② A Tudor coaching inn. The horses and coaches would be kept in the stables at the back.

▶ ③ The modern town of Ludlow, Shropshire, still has many Tudor buildings.

Inside a Tudor town house

What was it like inside a Tudor home? This depended on whether the house was added to or built from scratch.

There were many ways in which homes changed towards the end of Tudor times. But perhaps the most important change was the building of a brick fireplace and chimney.

The importance of a chimney

Without a chimney the upper part of the house filled with smoke and was unusable.

Cooking
Large fireplaces allow traditional cooking to take place, with cauldrons supported over an open fire.

Glass
Glass is now more affordable, and for the first time windows can be made bigger, letting more light into the rooms while keeping out the cold.

However, glass can't yet be made in large panes. To get over this problem the glass is stuck together with strips of lead. The result – leaded windows.

By 1600, many people could afford to buy bricks to make a fireproof chimney. This resulted in two important changes. First, the fire could be moved from the centre to the side of the room. Also, the smoke was kept out of the house and people could use the upper parts of their houses.

By adding a ceiling just above head height, houses could be divided into two floors for the first time. As a result, during Tudor times, people doubled the amount of usable space in their homes.

Parlours and bedrooms

So what did they do with their extra space? At the start of Tudor times, people slept downstairs in the **PARLOUR**.

But by the end of Tudor times, people were using their upstairs floor as bedrooms, leaving the downstairs parlour as a sitting room (picture ①).

◄ ① **A town-house parlour in late Tudor times. For a description of the furniture and fittings see pages 32 to 33.**

Beams
Beams used for walls and ceiling are still not covered over. Richer people use straight beams, but the less well off use tree branches.

Stairs
To get to the new upper floors, houses have a new feature – a staircase. It is steep and narrow so as not to use up more space than necessary.

Floors
Earth floors are boarded over and the floorboards raised on beams. This makes the house much warmer in winter.

Furniture and fittings

At the start of Tudor times, homes had little more than wood planks and a chest. By later Tudor times, people were buying proper tables and chairs.

In medieval times, before the Tudors, most people slept on planks of wood on the floor (picture ①) or used mattresses stuffed with straw. Only the very wealthy had beds.

Temporary tables would be made by placing sleeping boards on two trestles. Benches to sit on would be made of more planks and trestles. Only the very wealthy had proper tables and chairs.

In Tudor times, more people became wealthy enough to buy better furniture (picture ②). Our villagers tell us (from their wills; see box) about how important a change this was by describing their new furniture as 'joined up', meaning fixed permanently together. This could only be done because there was more room in the house (see pages 30–31).

What Tudor wills tell us

If you were wondering how we know so much about what people owned and did in our village, then the answer is that much of it is written in their wills.

By looking at the will of a craftsman like a skinner, we can find out about the contents of a typical Tudor house.

Our skinner left his son his clothes, including:

a coat, a pair of trousers, a bonnet (hat), cloak, doublet, sword and dagger, and a saddle.

In the house he left his wife:

two cooking pots, a plate, a pewter dish, a pair of candle-holders, a silver spoon, bowls, a tub for brewing beer, a barrel, a trencher (cutting board), and a set of scales and weights; a bed 'joined', a feather mattress and pillow, two pairs of sheets, blankets, a desk, a table 'joined', a cupboard, a long wooden seat, a bench, a chair, a spinning wheel and a chest.

When the skinner died, all his possessions were regarded as his – not his wife's. If he wanted his wife to have anything, he had to say so in his will.

▼ ① A bed in medieval times.

◄ ② A bed in late Tudor times. Most people thought their bed was their prize possession – even more so if it had a feather mattress.

Cooking

In the kitchen, villagers use metal cauldrons and other cooking pots hung over open fires from chains in fireplaces (picture ③). Metal spoons have been invented, but most people still eat from wooden platters (called trenchers) (picture ④), drink from wooden goblets or leather tankards (picture ⑤) and use wooden spoons at table. Forks have not been invented and people ate with natural forks – their fingers!

▲ ④ **Wooden trencher and spoon.**

▶ ⑤ **Leather tankard.**

Keeping clean

In our village, people are keeping themselves slightly cleaner. They have basins for washing in. Baths, though, are rare. People who have a bath every few months are thought of as exceptional. The richer villagers wear perfume to hide their own stench.

▼ ③ **Inside a Tudor kitchen.**

Smoked and salted meat

Corn grinding

Butter making

Storage jars and sacks

Joined-up table

Weblink: www.CurriculumVisions.com

What the Tudors ate and drank

The rich and poor Tudors ate very different foods.

We enjoy our food because we have the money to be able to choose what to buy. But few people had this luxury in Tudor times.

What the poor ate

The poor could afford only the simplest of foods. Bread formed a very important part of their diet. It had to be baked in the lord's oven, and for this he charged a fee.

White bread – made from wheat – was too expensive. Instead, poorer people ate a bread made from cheaper crops such as rye. This was dark brown and dense, and less pleasant to eat.

Most poor people also ate pottage, a stew made using oats with vegetables. Occasionally meat was added, perhaps pork, chicken or locally caught deer, boar and rabbits,

▼ ① Even though most Tudor people ate very simple food, they enjoyed their meals. This family are eating ryebread, fish and pottage, all washed down with weak beer.

which were considered the property of the lord of the manor. They also caught small fish from the river but only with the lord's permission.

If you were wealthy

The rich ate very well. Servants put out several courses on the table at the same time, so that diners could choose what order they wanted to eat them in.

Dishes were often very elaborate, using many spices, which had to be brought by ship from Asia or the Caribbean (see page 42).

Table manners

The wealthy washed their hands in public before eating. Everyone ate with their fingers from the same dishes. Good table manners included not putting their fingers in their ears, blowing their nose into their hands, or scratching during meals!

On the other hand, if they ate something with bones, it was considered quite polite to throw the bones onto the floor!

▼ ② The rich ate not only more food but also more varied and exotic food. Spread out on the table might be a roasted meat – perhaps venison or a capon – pastries stuffed with cod liver and a dish of chicken served in a spiced sauce of pounded crayfish tails.

Almshouse and workhouse

The Tudors had to find ways of dealing with the poor. They started with almshouses and ended with workhouses.

Towards the end of Tudor times, fewer people were needed to farm the land. As a result, some people found themselves without any land to work and no job. Other people were simply too young, old or frail to work and therefore had no income.

The Tudors thought differently about the poor according to whether they came from their own **PARISH** or from elsewhere.

Each parish was prepared to look after its own poor but didn't want poor people coming from outside. People were particularly afraid of **VAGRANTS**. These were people who wandered about in groups looking for work and who often stole as a way of staying alive.

Some people lived outside the law, robbing people who travelled along the roads. These people were called **VAGABONDS**.

The stocks – or worse – await

If people from outside the parish came begging they got a very hard time.

▼ ① Pillories were made of stout wood shaped to hold the head, arms and legs of a person due for punishment. Stocks had just two holes for legs.

People found guilty of a crime, such as vagrancy, were put on show to the whole village. The village constable could also give the offender a sound thrashing, while the villagers could pelt him with anything nasty they found on the roads – such as rotten fruit or horse dung.

One way people tried to discourage outsiders was to put them in the pillories or the stocks (picture ①). They were often whipped and could even be hanged.

Alms

Until the monasteries were destroyed by Henry VIII, the very poor were looked after by the Church. This kind of charity was called alms.

Wealthy people also sometimes left money in their wills to pay for special buildings to house the poor. These were almshouses and HOSPITALS (picture ②).

Workhouses

When the Church no longer did this job, government had to step in. At the end of Tudor times, government introduced a special tax called the Poor Rate. Its purpose was to provide for the old, sick, and infant poor.

The able-bodied, however, were forced to live in workhouses. These were buildings where people lived in exchange for hard work such as picking stones off the fields and filling in holes in the road.

The Tudor Poor Laws:

During Tudor times, the government made many laws dealing with the poor. The 'Poor Laws' distinguished two types of poor people: the deserving poor and vagrants.

The Deserving Poor

1495	Deserving poor may beg in own parish.
1536	People told to give money to church officials who will give to the most deserving
1538	Henry VIII takes over church lands.
1547	The parish must find homeless deserving poor a place to live. To help with this a collection for the poor is taken after church on Sunday.
1552	Licensed beggars may go from door to door in their own parish but they must not sit outdoors and beg.
1563	If people do not give money to the Sunday collection for the poor, they have to explain why not. If they don't have a good reason, they can be locked up.
1597	Overseers are appointed to look after the poor. The parish officials set a tax called the Poor Rate. If someone does not pay, the overseers can take their possessions and sell them to get the money.

Vagrants

1495	Vagrants to be punished in the stocks for 3 days.
1531	Vagrants to be whipped.
1536	Vagrants made to work on jobs like road repairs.
1547	Vagrants could be forced to work as slaves (this law was ended in 1549 because it was considered too harsh).
1572	Vagrants over 14 were to be whipped and have a hole made in their right ear the first time they were caught. Caught again, they could be put in prison or even hanged.
1576	Houses of Correction (workhouses) set up where vagrants were forced to live and work.
1597	Vagrants whipped and sent back to the county where they had last lived.

▲ ② This row of small dwellings was a hospital – a place for the aged poor built by a wealthy benefactor. No medicine was given there.

Plague

Rich and poor alike were likely to be struck down by disease. The only difference was whether you died in a comfortable bed or a hard one.

Tudor people had hard, often short lives. They usually had poor diets and lived in homes that were not kept clean.

This meant that diseases spread quickly. The most deadly disease was called **PLAGUE**. This had killed millions of people.

▼ ① Buildings were cramped and crowded, and no one cleared the rubbish from the streets. In these conditions it was easy for the plague to spread.

Plague is an infection caused by tiny organisms called **BACTERIA**. People usually get plague from being bitten by fleas carrying the plague bacteria. The fleas live in the fur of rats and mice.

In Tudor times, once a person was infected, there were no useful medicines to cure the plague, so both rich and poor died equally.

In the worst outbreaks of plagues, such as in Norwich in 1579, as much as 30 or 40 per cent of the population died.

The trouble with towns

Towns suffered from disease more than the countryside because they were more crowded and filthier. In crowded, unclean conditions it is easier for infections to spread.

How had this come about? It was all caused by the rapid growth of the town in Tudor times (see pages 28–29 and picture ①).

To cope with the demand for places to live, landlords built ramshackle houses of very poor quality. Whole families lived in one room, and several families shared a small two-storey tenement.

Everyone threw their waste into the gutters that ran down the centres of the roads. The waste materials attracted rats. As a result, both streets and homes were alive with rats.

When a plague broke out, all that could be done was to make sure the people and their families were shut in their homes. A red cross was painted on to their doors.

People were confined in their homes for five weeks. Watchmen gave them food, but made sure they did not get out. They either died or, if they were lucky, got better.

Learning

Learning gave the best chance of getting a good job in life – and even poor parents were prepared to pay for it.

▼ ① Schools taught only mathematics, Greek and Latin. If pupils did not behave they were whipped.

From Tudor times onwards, more and more people learned to write. In general, the wealthier you were, the greater your chances of being able to read and write. As a result, most wealthy people were able to read and write, but most peasants were not.

Families viewed the education of boys and girls differently. Most families educated the boys for work and the girls for marriage and running a household. Few girls learned subjects such as mathematics or foreign languages.

Foundations

To try to bring about more learning for the poor, the wealthy often left money for the foundation of schools (picture ②) as well as university colleges.

The Church

One of the best ways of getting on in life was to work for the Church. But to become a priest, you had to go to Oxford or Cambridge universities. If you paid them enough money, they gave you a degree. Only the wealthiest, therefore, became priests.

Grammar and local schools

The wealthiest people hired a private tutor (picture ①). Merchants, who could only afford to pay modest amounts, sent their sons to a grammar school or a school attached to a cathedral.

Poorer people, such as yeomen farmers, might occasionally be able to pay for their boys to go to a local school. However, when they were needed for sowing seed, lambing or harvesting crops, they did not go to school but worked on the farm instead.

Apprenticeships

Another way of learning was used by people who could not afford to send their children to any kind of school. This was called **APPRENTICESHIP**, and through it children learned a trade.

The only job you could get if you had not been apprenticed was to be a farm labourer or a servant. But if you learned a trade you could eventually hope to own your own business and so become wealthy.

In Tudor times, you might expect to be apprenticed as one of the following: glover, carpenter, chandler, skinner, fletcher, vintner, tailor, draper, saddler, cordmaker, tanner, walker, butcher, capper, dyer, (black)smith, barber, porter (who made beer), mercer and baker.

Parents were expected to pay for the teaching of the apprentice. An apprenticeship lasted for between five and seven years. Apprentices would live in the house of their master. There they got training, food and drink.

▼ ② A small schoolhouse of the kind founded by local wealthy people.

Exploration

Tudor times saw the first great explorations – and the first colonies.

Tudor times were part of a long period called the **AGE OF DISCOVERY**. It was a time when people from Europe sought new trade routes to the **SPICE ISLANDS** of Asia and by accident discovered new lands, which they then called their own.

Portugal and Spain had long sent out explorers, such as **CHRISTOPHER COLUMBUS**, to find the trade routes. These countries grew rich from the new lands they discovered. England knew that it had to join the race.

The passage to America

In 1496, King Henry VII gave permission for John Cabot and his sons to search for the Spice Islands by taking a northern route.

In May 1497, Cabot set sail from Bristol and reached Labrador or Newfoundland in Canada, although he thought he had reached China. This took the English to the Americas and gave them a stake in the New World.

▲ ① **Sir Francis Drake.**

But the greatest English exploration of all was led by another seaman, **SIR FRANCIS DRAKE**.

Drake: explorer and privateer

Drake was born about 1541, the son of a Devon tenant farmer. He began as an apprentice on boats in the stormy waters of the North Sea and here he learned his seaman's skills. Eventually, Drake became master of his own ship. One of Drake's relations was beginning to trade in the New World. Drake wanted to have his own adventures. He sold his own boat and enlisted as an officer in a fleet of boats crossing the Atlantic Ocean. During these voyages, Drake saw how the Spanish plundered the English ships. He was determined to avenge his country.

In 1572, Queen Elizabeth I agreed to allow Drake to become a **PRIVATEER** and attack the Spanish ships in the West Indies. He returned to England both rich and famous.

The Golden Hind

In 1577, Drake was chosen by the Queen as the leader of an expedition to the South Pacific. He set sail in December with five small ships, manned by fewer than 200 men. His flagship was called the *Pelican*, but he renamed it the *Golden Hind.*

By capturing Spanish ships and taking their treasure, the *Golden Hind* became loaded with bars of gold and silver, Spanish coins, precious stones, and pearls.

Around the globe

Drake next reached California, which he called New Albion. He was the first

▼ ② **Sir Francis Drake meets an Indian chief.**

European to sight the west coast of what is now Canada. From there, he went on to Asia.

On 26 September, 1580, Francis Drake brought his ship into Plymouth Harbour. He was the first captain ever to sail his own ship around the world. Queen Elizabeth rewarded him with a knighthood.

In 1596, Drake died of a fever while on an expedition to the West Indies and was buried at sea.

◀ ③ **Sir Francis Drake being knighted by Queen Elizabeth I.**

Weblink: www.CurriculumVisions.com

Settlers

Towards the end of Tudor times, English people began to set up colonies in the New World.

▲ ① **What the Roanoke colony might have looked like (a scattering of log cabins in evergreen forest).**

By the end of the 16th century, the English thought they had watched the Spanish and Portuguese gain **COLONIES** for long enough. It was time to act for themselves!

A new colony

In 1584, Queen Elizabeth I granted **SIR WALTER RALEIGH** a permit to colonise America.

Raleigh sent an expedition to explore possible places. His navigators, Philip Amadas and Arthur Barlow, returned to England with news of a supposed beautiful fertile island. This was Roanoke Island, which lies just off the coast of what is now North Carolina. In reality it was just a mosquito-infested swamp!

In 1585, using these reports, Raleigh decided to send out a group of a hundred families to found the first English settlement in North America.

▶ ③ The seal of the Virginia Company.

The 'Citie of Ralegh'

After the colonists arrived at the island of Roanoke, they began to build a town called 'Citie of Ralegh'. They soon got into trouble, however.

They found they could not clear enough land or grow enough food to live. So they had to trade with the local peoples (picture ①).

▼ ② John White founds the colony of Roanoke in 1587.

They quickly fell into arguments with the Native American peoples, and their supply of food was cut off. So, in 1586, they gave up and sailed back to England.

A second attempt

In 1587, Raleigh funded another group of colonists, under John White (picture ②) to go to Roanoke. The party included 90 men, 17 women, and 9 children.

After some weeks the colonists ran out of food. White sailed back to England for supplies, but didn't return until 1590. When he did get back, he found the houses were empty and there was no sign of the colonists.

Many must have died. Others may have joined with the Native Americans, while some may have tried their luck inland. Nobody knows what happened.

Success!

This story shows just how hard it was to set up a colony in a foreign land. It was not until 1607, just after the end of Tudor times, that the Virginia Company in London was able to found a permanent colony at Jamestown (picture ③).

Words, names and places

ABBEY An important and large church.

ABBOT The leader of an abbey.

AGE OF DISCOVERY The hundred years from the mid-15th to the mid-16th century when Europeans sought new trade routes with East Asia.

ANGLO-SAXONS The people who lived in England from the 5th to the 11th centuries and whose ancestors came from the land which is now Germany.

ANNE BOLEYN The second wife of King Henry VIII and mother of Queen Elizabeth.

APPRENTICESHIP A period of learning about a trade or craft through working with a master tradesman or craftsman.

ARMADA The great fleet sent by King Philip II of Spain in 1588 to invade England.

BACTERIA Microbes that can sometimes cause illness and possibly death if they get into the human body.

BAILIFF An official of the court who carries out punishments.

CATHERINE OF ARAGON First wife of King Henry VIII and mother of Queen Mary.

CHRISTOPHER COLUMBUS The man widely called the 'discoverer' of the New World (the Americas). He was a master navigator and admiral for the Spanish king.

COLONIES Settlements in conquered territories.

CUTLER A craftsman who makes cutlery (knives and spoons).

DISSOLUTION OF THE MONASTERIES The closure and sometimes the destruction of the monasteries carried out by Henry VIII from 1538.

DOUBLET A close-fitting jacket.

EDWARD VI The only legitimate son of Henry VIII. He was born to Jane Seymour, Henry's third wife. He reigned for six years (1547 to 1553).

ELIZABETH I Queen of England and daughter of Henry VIII and Anne Boleyn. Known as The Virgin Queen and Good Queen Bess, she reigned between 1558 and 1603 during a time when England was rising as a world power.

ENCLOSURE The taking over of farm- or pastureland by local landlords.

GALLEON A large sailing ship used for war or trade.

GREAT REBUILDING The time during the late Tudor period when some people became wealthy enough to build bigger and better houses.

HENRY VII The first of the Tudor kings. He reigned from 1485 to 1509.

HENRY VIII King of England from 1509 to 1547. He had six wives: Catherine of Aragon (the mother of Queen Mary I), Anne Boleyn (the mother of Queen Elizabeth I), Jane Seymour (the mother of King Edward VI), Anne of Cleves, Catherine Howard and Catherine Parr.

HOSE Tight fitting woollen 'tights' worn by men.

HOSPITAL A place where the elderly poor were given hospitality – board and lodging. It usually took the form of a row of small terraced houses.

LATH A strip of wood used in building a house.

LEPER A person suffering from a disease called leprosy that affects the skin. It was one of the most feared diseases of Tudor times.

LORD OF THE MANOR A nobleman who owned a large area of land called a manor.

MARY I Also called Mary Tudor, she was the first queen to rule England (1553–1558). Her aim was to bring back the Roman Catholic faith to England.

MARY, QUEEN OF SCOTS Also called Mary Stuart, Queen of Scotland. Mary inherited Tudor blood through her grandmother, a sister of Henry VIII. She was eventually beheaded on the orders of Elizabeth I as a Roman Catholic threat to the English throne.

MEDIEVAL TIMES The period that lasted from the fall of the Roman Empire in the 5th century AD until Tudor times.

MONASTERY A religious house of prayer and learning. Usually the home of monks.

NORMAN TIMES The period following the conquest of England by William I in 1066 which lasted through the 11th and 12th centuries.

PARISH A small area – often a village and its surroundings.

PARLOUR A room used for entertaining guests.

PEASANT A person who worked the land in exchange for a proportion of the produce that was grown.

PLAGUE An infectious disease carried by fleas that live on rats.

PLASTER A paste of lime water and sand that hardens on drying and used for coating walls and ceilings.

PRIVATEER Someone who runs a private armed ship and who has a licence to attack enemy ships.

PROTESTANT A person belonging to a Christian movement that arose in the 16th century; it broke with the teachings of the Roman Catholic Church.

ROMAN CATHOLIC CHURCH The Christian Church that dominated western Europe from early medieval times. Its leader was the pope, whose home was in Rome.

SIR FRANCIS DRAKE An English admiral most noted for sailing around the world between 1577 and 1580. He also played an important role in defeating the Spanish Armada in 1588.

SIR WALTER RALEIGH Seaman and adventurer, and a favourite of Queen Elizabeth I, who knighted him in 1585.

SPICE ISLANDS A group of islands in South East Asia, famous for their spice such as nutmeg and cloves. Today they are called the Moluccas.

STEWARD A person who managed the day to day affairs of a nobleman.

TITHE A tenth part. A form of tax during medieval times.

TUDOR Kings and queens belonging to the house of Tudor which began with Henry VII and ended with Elizabeth I. Also, the English people living at this time.

VAGABOND A person who would attack travellers for their belongings and money.

VAGRANT A person with no fixed home.

VIKINGS People of the early medieval times who had their homeland in Scandinavia and who raided England from the end of the 8th century. Several kings of England during this time were Vikings.

WATTLE AND DAUB A simple way of making walls by plaiting willow branches into a sheet and then covering the frame with a mixture of mud, dung and straw.

WEST INDIES Islands in the Caribbean Sea, off the east coast of central America.

WILLIAM SHAKESPEARE World-famous Elizabethan playright. He was born about 1564 in Stratford-upon-Avon and died April 23, 1616.

WILLIAM THE CONQUEROR Also called William I. A duke of Normandy who attacked England in 1066 to battle for his claim to the English throne. He ruled from 1066 to 1087.

YEOMAN A rich farmer.

Index

abbey 8, 12, 18, 19, 22, 23, 46
abbot 12, 18, 46
Age of Discovery 42, 46
alms 37
almshouse 36, 37
Anglo-Saxons 10, 11, 46
apprenticeship 41, 46
Armada 5, 24–25, 46

bacteria 39, 46
bailiff 14, 46
baker 14, 19, 41
barn 10, 26
bed 31, 32, 38
beer 15, 32, 34
beermaker (brewer) 15, 18, 19, 32, 41
Boleyn, Anne 22, 46
brick 20, 27, 30, 31
brickmaker 18, 19
butcher 14, 19, 41

Cabot, John 42
candlemaker 15, 19
castle 8, 9, 10, 11, 20
Catherine of Aragon 22, 46
ceiling 13, 27, 31
chimneys 10, 12, 13, 20, 29, 30, 31
Church, the 5, 12, 16, 22–23, 37, 41
church 10, 11, 14
Citie of Ralegh 45
clothes 6–7, 18, 21, 32
colonies 42, 44–45, 46
Columbus, Christopher 5, 42, 46
cooking 30, 33
court of law 14
cutler 19, 46

Deserving Poor 37
disease 8, 13, 29, 38–39
Dissolution of the monasteries 5, 22–23, 46
doublet 7, 32, 46
Drake, Sir Francis 5, 24–25, 42–43, 47
drink 15, 33, 34, 41

East India Company 5
education 40–41
Edward VI 4, 5, 24, 46
Elizabeth I 4, 5, 24, 26, 42, 43, 44, 46
enclosure 17, 46
exploration 42–43

farming 11, 16–17, 36, 41
fire, open 13, 20, 30, 31, 33
fireplace 13, 30, 33
fireships 25
floors 11, 12, 13, 14, 19, 21, 27, 31, 35
food 5, 13, 18, 24, 34–35, 41

forest 8, 9, 11, 13, 44
furniture 32–33

galleon 24, 46
gallery 21
garden, kitchen 11, 13, 18, 29
glass 20, 29, 30
Golden Hind 43
Great Rebuilding 26–27, 46

hall house 10, 11, 12
Hampton Court 20
Henry VII (Henry Tudor) 4, 5, 8, 42, 46
Henry VIII 4, 5, 6, 20, 22, 24, 37, 46
hose 7, 46
hospital 37, 46
house 5, 10–11, 12–13, 17, 18–19, 20–21, 23, 26–27, 28, 29, 30–31, 32–33

inn 18, 19, 28, 29

lath 13, 46
learning 40–41
leper 19, 46
lord of the manor 12, 35, 46

market 11, 14, 15, 19, 18, 28
Mary I 4, 5, 24, 46
Mary, Queen of Scots 5, 47
medieval times 10, 32, 47
merchant 18, 19, 23, 41, 28
mill 11, 14, 18
monastery 5, 22, 37, 47

New World (North America) 5, 42, 44–45
night soil carriers 19
Norman times 11, 47

parish 36, 37, 47
parlour 31, 47
path 11, 15
peasant 5, 12, 16, 17, 40, 47
pillories 15, 36, 37
plague 38–39, 47
plaster 13, 47
poor 5, 6–7 and throughout
Poor Rate 37
pope 22
potter 18, 19
priest 41
privateer 42, 47
Protestant 5, 22, 24, 47

Raleigh, Sir Walter 5, 44–45, 47
rats 13, 39

rich 5, 6–7 and throughout
river 8, 9, 10, 14, 18, 19, 35
road 10, 15, 28, 29, 37, 39
Roanoke Island 44–45
Roman Catholic Church 5, 22, 47
Royal Navy 24
rubbish 15, 38. See also Waste
ruff 6, 7

school 40–41
servant 20, 21, 35, 41
settlers 44–45
Shakespeare, William 5, 47
sheep 8, 16
skinner 19, 32, 41
Spain 24, 25, 42
Spice Islands 42, 47
St James Palace 20
starvation 5, 8
steward 14, 47
stocks 36, 37
stone 5, 20, 23, 27
strip fields 8, 11, 16, 18

tailor 19, 41
tanner 15, 18, 19, 41
tithe 12, 47
toilet 14, 15, 29
town 5, 17, 18–19, 21, 28–29, 39, 45
town hall 28
town house 21, 30–31
trades 14–15, 19, 41
trading 5, 42, 45
Tudor, definition of 47

vagabond 36, 47
vagrant 36, 37, 47
village 8–9, 10–11, 12–13, 14–15, 26–27, 36
village hall 14
Vikings 10, 47
Virginia Company 45

washing 33, 35
waste 11, 39. See also Rubbish
water, running 29
wattle and daub 11, 13, 47
weaver/weaving 13, 14, 19
West Indies 24, 42, 43, 47
White, John 45
will 32, 37
William the Conqueror 8, 47
wool 5, 7, 16
work 5, 14, 17, 18, 28, 36, 37, 40, 41. See also trades
workhouse 36, 37
workshop 19, 28
yeoman 11, 12, 16, 17, 27, 41, 47